CONDITION OF FIRE

Condition of Fire

JL WILLIAMS

Shearsman Books
Exeter

First published in the United Kingdom in 2011 by
Shearsman Books
58 Velwell Road
Exeter EX4 4LD

http://www.shearsman.com/

ISBN 978-1-84861-145-0

Acknowledgements

These poems were written on the isle of Salina, one of the volcanic
Aeolian Islands off the coast of Sicily in the Tyrrhenian Sea, said to be
the home of the god of winds.
Utmost gratitude to the Scottish Arts Trust, Robyn Marsack and to
Edwin Morgan for the Edwin Morgan Travel Bursary that made this
journey possible.

Contents

for RJ Iremonger   mea lux

But certainly it is always to the Condition of Fire, where emotion is not brought to any sudden stop, where there is neither wall nor gate, that we would rise; and the mask plucked from the oak-tree is but my imagination of rhythmic body. We may pray to that last condition by any name so long as we do not pray to it as a thing or a thought, and most prayers call it man or woman or child.

W.B. Yeats, *Anima Mundi*

Now that it's all finally in the past,
it seems almost as if you gave yourself
to those desires too—how they glowed,
remember, in eyes that looked at you,
remember, body, how they trembled for you in those voices.

C.P. Cavafy, *Body, Remember . . .*
translated by Edmund Keeley & Philip Sherrard

Note to reader

Many of the stories and all of the lists are drawn from Ovid's *Metamorphoses*.

Black Island in the Dusk

Who is the intruder?

Before it was sunrise
but now it is sunset that reminds
me I am alive.

A handful of fire.

0

Make the shape of a zero with your fingers.
Hold this shape to your eye.
Look out onto the black sea,
the black shore.

Remote Beginning

I

Life that rises from the core of the earth,
leaks from the lips of stone,
boils the mountain's skin,
enters the sea.

Light in the sky at night, fire in the leaves.

Uvula of the chaos stretched to a thread.

White light spreading over the surface of sea.

Two rocks watch the light, have the faces of men.

A place from which movement begins,
skeleton of flames.

Bells in a stone tower,
the fire, the womb.

The tongue.
The flame.
The star.

THE END OF BELIEF.

II

The bat, its face a plum warmed by the sun.

The tongue is the root of the flame.

He exhales. His body sinks,
a plug of lead in a carcanet of fish.
They enter into his nose, his mouth,
they fill up his ears.
He reaches out   out   is a school of fish
ducking this way, that way toward shallower water.

III

It was made from fire (she opens her mouth).

TIME

comes out,
crashes the sky,
threshing the breasts of her children.

I am sorry for in truth I am better than this;
a waterfall of fire in a place with no gravity.

Imago

He thought of so many ways to make this
(veined wing, weightless thing),
walked in nothingness dreaming.

Gathered and tossed stars like coins or
(gold, glass)
marbles.

The stars weren't anything.

He decided to separate first
earth sky sea land heaven air
(heavy earth, light heaven),
let them find their places
in and round the world.

How he enjoyed the splashing sound
(azure, periwinkle, emerald, cobalt, violet, cornflower, blue)
that snaked and pooled and froze, in places, rose.

The winds, his children, he banished each to their rooms.

The sea made fish, the air birds, the heavens gods, the land beasts
and man was moulded by Prometheus, who found in mud
flakes of scattered stars, and wetting them in rivers shaped
creatures with eyes looking upwards, who walked dreaming.

Drowning

I

She dies but there is no trace of her on the radar.
The bat's voice echoes back
tension of sea.

Below, weed-coated rocks.
Like caterpillars, fish
hack a mouthful, chew, take no notice.

II

I want another word for dying –
change is good.

For beginnings to exist
there must be change.

We can explain things via change,
make loss gain.

III

I had hands,
then they were fins.
Sometimes, wings.

Watch the bat.
Watch the fish underwater.

I swam with a rock in my hand.

When I took it out of the water,
it wept.

Proserpine says,

I want to tell you seven things about dying.

The first is that some people do come back.

Death makes changes happen to the living.

Mothers never recover from the death of their children.

Death is capable of love.

Of death fruit grows.

The dead that partake inure themselves to death.

It is colours you will miss when you are dead.

Tide and Time

The rolling voice of God throws me
back on the sand.

My hands in crabs' reach.

What steels me, pinions
the bones to the cleft of the wave?

Boatless, I dive in again.

Lingua

The bat flies
listening
always to its own reflection.

Coral

Below the teal blue
surface of water white
stones like knees.

Snake heads dance
as the mouth of the Gorgon
steels moonlight.

Nimble, nymphs carry
armfuls of weed to the rock
where Medusa cries,

laughing and
keeping their faces
turned toward the sea.

Phæton

Boy leaves his mother's arms.

Boy embarks on desert, falls to sand.
Boy sees the sun.
Boy sees his father's face.

Boy insists, "Let me hold the reins!"

Lightning sparks the sky.
Flames boil sea.
Fishes roast in all the world's waves.

Far out in space
stars open their mouths and scream.

Boy dies as his father burns, helpless.

His mother makes a wish on a falling star.

Helios Retires

How pale the sea,
the pale of rain in pools.

Will the doors with the white whales ever be opened?
Will the horses that pull the sun
ever be harnessed?

Proserpine Under a Tree

What if you could change?
Most of the ones changed into trees wept sap.
Some bled as their mothers tore off bark.

Some were rescued by being turned into trees.
Some were granted the gift of being turned
along with lovers to flower arm-in-arm.

Some were caught in trees and never freed,
some learned to change subtly in Autumn,
Spring.

What if you could change into anything?
What if you could live, and live, and live?

Volcano

Last night the mouth of the earth spewed up fire.

One girl said she felt strange, her limbs heavy.
She said her blood, "felt like turning into honey."

When she burst into blossom we were on the volcano.
Her cry was more like a trumpet, it came out of mouth
turning from mouth into petalled coronet.

The end of it was nothing
but the tremble of a white flower on a vine.

Ovid's Demands

Give me a handful of fire.

It will not kill me.

Give me the Sun's chariot.

It will not kill me.

Give me the snake-infested head.

It will not kill me.

Give me the hoof of the bull.

It will not kill me.

Give me the Golden Fleece.

It will not kill me.

Give me the pomegranate seed.

It will not kill me.

Give me the chalice of gods.

It will not kill me.

Give me your blessing.

Give me your blessing.

Give me your blessing.

Condition of Fire

I

Lesson

And I asked, what is fire?
And you replied by putting my hand
on the hob to teach me.

You were always teaching us,
weren't you,
what it meant to burn?

II

Substance

Deep under the water its colour changed
but it was still
anemone, a budding flame.

III

Dessert

In a bowl of ice, an orange flower.

Remember, how as we walked past windows,
my reflection could burn fingers?

How you would keep in your mouth always this,
fire, and my other name.

Io

Like many teenage girls it took
disaster for Io to realise
she was beautiful.

Zeus turned her into a cow
to hide from his wife
he'd been raping innocent girls.

Io is a stunning cow.
Her father holds her soft face in his hands,
torn by relief and wishing she'd never been born.

Herse's Wedding Day

Aglauros can hardly breathe for the barbed wire.
Her sister's happy face swims before her eyes.

Minerva shudders as she clambers from the gutter;
Envy's half-eaten snakes writhe at her ankles.

Mercury tucks a hyacinth into his lapel
walking toward Herse's door past poor Aglauros,
now a statue of Aglauros.

Deaf Bat

The bat once had a long nose.

He flew many times into walls,
became a better listener.

Marsyas

Having no room for his instrument,
having to leave it behind he'd been going mad;
drumming the side of the boat, humming under his breath.

When he saw the thing hanging he didn't think twice;
pulled it out of the branches, began to play.

We hardly saw what did it, just a flash.

His heart, now visible,
beats in time to the tune.

A winged creature flies toward the sun,
his entire skin in its mouth
like a paper doll.

Metamorph

So many turned to birds or rivers.

A woman dissolved in tears.

Sisters falling through sky
on sudden wings.

Beach

Ching, ching, a delicate ringing
accompanies each step.

When stars came to pieces, fire wrought holes
in bones of ore.

They burn our naked feet
but we walk slowly.

History

Lately we notice our shadows
lighter round the edge.

The prophetess said,
"The danger is in knowing."

From our mouths,
burning the lips, fire.

Our trailing conversation;
essays of soot.

Wasp's Nest

The statues in the cemetery
are full of life.

One, ravaged by lichen,
lifts her face.

Another raises a handful of wasps
higher than the crown of its wings.

The Audience of Orpheus

Durmast
Poplar
Oak
Lime
Laurel
Beech
Ash
Hazel
Fir
Ilex
Maple
Plane
Willow
Water-lotus
Box
Tamarisk
Myrtle
Viburnum
Ivy
Vine
Elm
Pitch-pine
Mountain-ash
Arbutus
Palm
Pine

Orpheo

The best audience of all was the trees.

They just listened.

I thought of them
as I was torn to pieces.

I thought of their stillness.

Threnody

When Eurydice was alive, did he sing for her?
Did the birds gather then, and the deer,
and all the gods and goddesses,
folks round about,
to hear his song of love for Eurydice?

Was it a lack of trust lost Eurydice,
or merely love so strong it couldn't wait
but turned, and turned, and turned
(never-ending refrain)
Eurydice back into a ghost?

It is said Eurydice never complained,
but limped away again into darkness
while Orpheus begged, and screamed,
and hungered, and sang
a sadder song than even the one before.

Eurydice's Matter

It is her body that troubles;
one minute shade, but limping, physical—
whole again, nearly flesh,
then going like smoke at the edges
back into death.

When Orpheus finally dies,
ripped apart by Maenads,
pieces of him do not rain on the Underworld.

He searches wildly, runs to her,
lifts her in his arms.

He is whole again,
but he does not sing.

He walks a little ahead and she behind,
often turning to watch her
limping through flowers.

Aesacus

Of all women, she the only one.

He chased her through the woods he knew so well.

Now he feels sorry, so sorry, so very sorry.

Changed he is, though inside he is still

confused as before, a bird condemned to dive

and swim and rise and, not fly—fall.

Sanctus

Sleep may be the most beautiful god of all,
in his poppy-strewn house with no doors to creak,
no servants to speak,
just dreams without passengers
floating past a dusky bed on which he nods.

Kingfisher

If love is a kind of fire
why didn't it save Ceyx from glacial waves?

Alcyone waking from a dream
as his dead body returns to where it departed.

Alcyone building a nest
of bones that float on the sea better than ships.

Foundling

I

We looked for you everywhere.
We climbed the citadel.

There you were, among ruins,
throwing rocks.

II

Who lived here?
Whose hand built this wall, this doorway,
this castle for winds?

III

I watch you swimming by the rocks.
Your head is visible, then not. Then again I see
the features impressed on my heart.

IV

The winds live here.

You hear them
in long grass.

V

We do not approach you,
we wait for you to come.

It is better this way, as all around
are steep cliffs and below
waves crashing on rocks.

Ovid's Child

I can't remember much talk of cocoons.
His changes come more quickly, made by gods.

Sometimes falling,
suddenly,
feathers instead of fingers ply the wind.

Or running one trips, tries
to rise—foot caught in soil,
brushes tears from eyes but leaves flutter by.

Once a son born of a trunk,
you could say by Love.

Actæon's Dogs

Aello
Agre
Alce
Argiodus
Asbolus
Canache
Cyprius
Dorceus
Dromas
Harpalus
Harpyia
Hylactor
Hylaeus
Ichnobates
Labros
Lachne
Lacon
Ladon
Laelaps
Leucon
Lycisce
Melampus
Melanchaetes
Melaneus
Nape
Nebrophonus
Oresitrophos
Oribasus
Pamphagus
Poemenis
Pterelas
Sticte
Theridamas
Theron
Thoos
Tigris

Tongues of Fire

Speak.

Words burn a path of ash—
obsidian slides glassy as the back of a fish.

Search for food, for wood,
for land not covered in bones.

Change, quickly,
into other things.

Move on with wings, tusks, stranger things.
Unspeakable things.

Burning mouths.

In Vino Veritas

To Bacchus, conceived of Jove's (mother killing) fire
and born of his thigh, to burn in every
woman's heart and mouth of man who swallows the blood
          of the grape.

Slain by Ulysses

Caenaros
Chromius
Alastor
Alcander
Halius
Noemon
Prytanis
Charops
Thoon
Chersidamas
Ennomos

Hecuba

She was slender.

She had been queen and a queen's grace
raised her head as if it wore a crown.

Watching her brave daughter sacrificed,
seeing her last son's
corpse of enormous wounds,
many said
it was she who should have been blinded.

Her silver hair,
smoke from her children's pyres.

No rings left on her hand
of so great a fortune.

Still she holds her head up.
Still the old bitch growls, fights all comers.

Ash Birds

Risen of ash, risen of the son of Dawn,
we fight to the death to honour his warring soul.

Like Cadmus' sons, a race of men
born from the teeth of the snake,
whose first and last breaths were the same,
we rise and fight and die with the fire on his corpse.

Open our wings of ash,
spread our cries of ash,
fall in sprays of ash.

The mother of Memnon weeps,
and all the ash-strewn world runs with ink.

Thebes

I

We know this kind of thirst—
saltwater looks drinkable.

The goats are raw round their ankles
pulling at ropes.

We know this kind of smoke—
the sort from pyres.

One daughter with a second mouth,
one impaled on her shuttle.

All we can see is smoke.
It increases thirst.

II

&tc

volcano bees

snake stick

virgin sacrifice, city of grief

fires, fires of Troy

The Sibyl of Cumae

I

All things fall but some not soon enough.

If you wake with death in your mouth,
the ashen taste,
and your family before your eyes
buried or burned, remember the Sibyl
alive as many years
as grains of dust,
but with no youth for centuries.

Her first wish to live forever,
her wish for so long after
merely to die.

II

I have seen my beauty go
the way of civilisation.

What are years to me?
Grains of dust in a jar.

I never gave up my principles—
that I don't regret.

But having watched so many die,
I cannot help but wonder at all this love.

Banshee

The storm raged all night.

Morning sees tents blown over,
water in the fire pits and
giant boulders washed down the vanished path.

One is missing,
the lighter of the fires.

Four monstrous footprints leading up the mountain,
the last one deepest,
as if pushed off for flight.

Picus the Pecker

Circe is a spoiled child.

Where she walks tigers and lions mew like kittens,
maidens sort pallid flowers, disgusted pigs shriek.

Whatever she touches is hers, is changed,
is broken.

What sort of love makes you look ridiculous?

My precious wife sings a lament to rival Orpheus
while I bash this tree with my hammerhead beak,
picturing Circe's face.

Shadow and Lichen

I

It doesn't hurt.

It's a bit like breathing out,
and not having to breathe in.

One minute I was flesh then
the way smoke drifts off fire,
mist a field as sun rises,
clouds of dust from the bare feet of a runner
settle, I was shadow and
shadow with you remain.

II

It didn't happen all at once.

When I washed the sink's basin would be
tinged with green like a fish tank left to slime,
my body becoming moss over time from the outside in—
the tiny hairs on me turning to minute stem-like leaves and
eventually even veins and organs unfolding in
slow clumps of lichen.

Slow. Slow. Now everything is
slow as can be, as if time
has come to a halt and
the passing of each day takes
what seems like eternity.

Cunta Fluunt, Endless Flux

One had a shadow for a face
and an overgrown fedora.

One had a bird-face or bird-mask,
difficult to tell.

They were in the room but distance
was impossible to calculate.

Above the bed but not in a place
was a hole that led

to what I cannot say.

As I watched they seemed
to change their places or bodies,

both individual entities but
one was sometimes one, one the other.

I got the impression
theirs was one sort of change,

the hole another. Pythagoras writes:
moths are born of graves.

Lux Aeterna

Couldn't smell at first,
then it was a sea chest finally opened.

Legs entwined. Familiar;
even though these are new bodies.

We realise; the light won't die,
though everything is dark.

Like Myrmidons

The ants live up to their tough reputation but
have undergone a change—doltish, winged,

they rise from cracks: a plague of confused thoughts
crashing our faces, handfuls then hundreds and hundreds.

We brush them off gently, not killing one.
For each gross, tiny miracle is a score against apocalypse.

Lizard

The change is small, not deadly, oft repeated.

A little knob remains like a black bullet.

The tail grows back and

the lizard gets smarter.

Some of us break apart and grow together,

while some lay in pieces,

drift off in the rain.

Romulus' Point

There are many ways of claiming place
but to own it you must plant;
the seed of a Caesar,
a spear bursting into leaf.

Warning

A girl swims in rough water,
surf tossing rocks.

One massive wave rolls
her over her own
head and into
another form; seahorse, curl-tailed.

Morphemes

The snake is becoming of the tree's arm.

Gold bees swarm the volcano's lip.

The sea's noise
is the speeches of drowning stones.

Daphne

She hides her face in leaves.

His hot thighs
rub her trunk,
her torn dress
tangled in the roots of the tree.

Pilgrims

All sound at once is the same as silence.
All colour at once is the same as black.

We are brands of fire
on a shuddering breast.

Punished

I

Actæon never meant to find perfection.

Stumbling through the undergrowth,
cursing his own eyes,

torn apart by hounds
as his friends call,

"Actæon,
Actæon—we've caught one!"

the stag weeps.

II

Secretly, behind the rage,
was pleasure in her blush?

Metamorphoses

Ages Golden to Iron
Stable ground to sea
Ocean to dry land
Plain to a valley
Marsh to a dune
Dry wilderness to a swamp
Rivers burst and dry
Rivers sweet become tainted
Islands become land-locked, land islands
Plains become hills
Springs change hot to cold
Waters light fires
Waters turn guts to stone
Waters tint hair gold
Waters change men's minds
Volcanoes burn and sleep
Water makes men grow feathers
A dead bull will bear bees
A buried horse will give hornets
A buried crab's claw will birth a scorpion
Buried grubs will yield butterflies
Frogs come from mud, grow legs
Bears lick their cubs into shape
Bee maggots grow wings
Birds come from eggs
The marrow in a dead man's spine births snakes
The phoenix births itself from its own ash

Æolus

He says, "I am the wind,
this is my island."

He throws flowers
into the air with his voice.

Bat

Each evening he paints his face
black with ash.

The smell is like wet wood
or a sack in the rain.

He doesn't even open
his eyes anymore.

His wings are oilskin
stretched between fingers.

Each morning I see the marks
where he has been.

Treasure

On the bottom of every ocean
scattered like so many stars;
coins with the faces of men.

Burial

For the first five hundred years
ash remains in pots.

Then slowly the wind and water
take the ash.

Ash drifts off in sleep.
Ash flows in streams.

The ash is a message to all;
uncertain flag.

We stand on the bows of our ships
in the absence of man.

It is not true
in the end there is only ash.

Daedalus Considers

The last picture I took was of his fine shoulders.

Most of what you can see is blue-bright ocean.

Maybe only gods can make birds of men.

Sometimes I think it wasn't that he couldn't hear me,

but rather that he wished to experience change.

Convincing Erysichthon's Daughter

It's not so often I see you like this—
whole.

Usually it's as a dog's tail wagging with a goat's mouth
munching weed, bird falling toward the water's lip
fins unfolding, dark tipping into light the way
a rock holds back the beam before
blind sunshine.

Your father could sell you a hundred, thousand times
and never be full.

Why become whatever he can get a price for?

He will make a meal of himself,
looks already at his toes as if they were sausage.

Come with me now.

You can be anything; a waterfall, a woman.

Alcidamas' Daughter

It was her father thought it strange
when wings unfolded from between her legs.

The boys rejoicing anyway
with vats of wine and man-making play.

She held damp feathers,
black eyes and saw

trees swaying in a breeze;
the breath of her lover,

or the turning of the earth.

Last Winds

I

Will you walk as soon as the sun rises?

The ships are ready at dock.
The tar is hard.

The heavy sails do not move in the wind.

Will you walk as slow as you are able?

II

It is sad to watch the boats.
What was it he said?

"Our forefathers are buried."

They founded that church,
their names are in this book.

He offered me
the boots of his dead mother

who used to watch
the sails fall off the world.

Anemochory

If you met yourself
having come back in time
and offered some good advice
gleaned from your long life and all
its contretemps

would you find yourself with each word
changed, your own self
rippled by every
whistle of knowledge?

And would there come a sense
of what it is to be
spreader and seed?

The wing and also
wind?

Those of Water

We find that as we break the light
comes up from an unsuspected centre.

Sometimes we lie down to feel
we are not moving backward.

But the other thing is that, on the ground,
the wind in the grass sounds as if it is speaking.

Like Numa's Wife, Water Remembers

Nymph whose sorrow melts you into pools,
why does Proserpine's rape make you so unhappy?

Was she as sad, wandering the dark forest?

And thanks to him
does she not know rebirth?

A return to rather than exit from the mother.

Sometimes all the ways we were injured trouble us;
like freezing in winter the water remembers
shattering and trembles but flows on.

Vita Nova

The stag jumps over a house,
lands as a woman, falls,
turns into a stag.

The fish is two parts mortal:
head; food,
belly; food.

The third part is immortal:
return to the river.

Scales fall,
fall,
become light.

Maggots crawl out of a dead horse;
little white fingers
pointing at the sky.

Caesar's Balcony

There is silence, when there is dust in the air and the army is
      riding away
and then the sound of footsteps on water
coming from the other direction, from where
the water begins.

There is the sound of a mountain pushing trees out of rocks
and over there, the sound of a sword parting water.

There is the jingling harness of a pair of black horses
and budding amphibians opening
rubber horns of throats.

There is the place wherein radical changes occur;
contorted autumnal mutations, leaves being other things

and this in between
silence

and over there, on the run, history.

Apotheosis

In darkness,
beaten by moths,
you realise you are the light.

The body wrapped in cotton
marked on the nipples and pubis.

All you are is this picture.

Lay the body on wet sand;
octopi slither its belly.

The heart in the mouth of the owl.

How many bulbs have you shattered
making a death for yourself?

No apology for transformation.

In deep water,
a voice vibrating sunk lines.

Turned over, the body is still desirable.

Where do hands go
when there is no time?

The eyes of this one have no bottom.

As if the well pennies
could save face,

tapestry slowly becomes moth.

In darkness,
stared at by the starving,
you realise you are the fire.

Time is our Dream of the World

All that is left of a city
buried in ash.

Lightning Source UK Ltd.
Milton Keynes UK
UKOW051434020712

195353UK00001B/16/P